HOCKEY MOMS AREN'T CRAZY!

by
Jody M. Anderson,
artwork by Scott Rolfs

Big Pond Books
an imprint of Lake 7 Creative, LLC
Minneapolis, Minnesota

The jokes in this book came from my own experiences raising three hockey players. I also borrowed ideas from many of my Hockey Mom friends, who so willingly shared them with me. I rounded out the book by putting a new spin on some of those old and retold jokes we've heard a hundred times before. I would like to thank my family, friends, players, coaches, trainers, and all who shared Hockey Mom memories that made this book possible. I would also like to thank Big Pond Books for believing in my project. Without you, none of this would've happened!

The illustrations in this book were drawn from the imagination of Scott Rolfs. Any resemblance to real persons, living or dead, is purely coincidental.

Book edited and designed by Ryan Jacobson

10 9 8 7 6 5 4 3 2

Library of Congress Control Number: 2013936339

Copyright 2013 by Jody M. Anderson
Published by Big Pond Books
an imprint of Lake 7 Creative, LLC
Minneapolis, MN 55412
www.bigpondbooks.com

ISBN: 978-0-9883662-1-3

This book is dedicated to all Hockey Moms, everywhere!

—Jody M. Anderson

Foreword

My mom was the perfect Hockey Mom, and that's why she's a great candidate to write this book. I played hockey for ten years, and my mom barely ever missed a game. I think she might have been more dedicated than I was! My mom was my biggest supporter, bringing me to morning practices at 5:30 a.m., always pushing me to do my best, and never letting me give up.

It was my senior year, and I was having a really tough year. I didn't know if I wanted to keep playing, but my mom told me to keep going. I don't know what I would've done without my mom during hockey. She did everything possible to keep me positive.

I want to thank her for never giving up on me and never letting me give up on hockey. Love ya mom!

—Katie Anderson,
Hockey Daughter

An Introduction

When my son Jeremy was in the second grade, he came home with a paper for hockey sign-up at the local school. He was so excited; how could I say no? Little did I know it would lead to a life of volunteering to bring treats, becoming the hockey manager, writing the bylaws & articles of incorporation for the girls' high school team . . . We also gained a lifelong obsession with hockey!

As I reflect back on my life as a Hockey Mom, I remember all the family time we spent together and all the friends we made. At the end of every season, we always had a parents-versus-kids game. It was a blast. Those kids played harder against us than they did all year! (It's still always a debate about who won those games.)

Of course, if there's one thing about Hockey Moms, it's that we have stories. I've shared so many tales about hockey, the kids, the coaches, and the tournaments that one day someone said, "You need to write a book!"

After thinking about it for a while, I decided it was a great idea. But not just for me. I wanted to make a tribute to all Hockey Moms out there.

I started sharing book ideas with other moms, which led to interviews not only with Hockey Moms but also with the players themselves. They seemed to relish the opportunity to say how important their Hockey Moms were—and still are—to them. Next, I took my idea to social media, and I got a lot of positive responses.

I was on Twitter one night, and a tweet by Mike Eruzione (perhaps most famously known as the captain of the 1980 Winter Olympics United States national hockey team) alerted me that he happened to be on, too. So I thought, "What the heck? I'll zap him a tweet and see if I can get a story or two about his mom." I told him about the book and that I'd love to include a story about his mom. He got right back to me and said yes; I was shocked!

Two days later, Mike Eruzione called me, and I about had a heart attack. He wanted to do the interview right then and there, but I told him I was in no way prepared for him! He was very understanding, and we set up an appointment for a later time. I then proceeded to drive to an eye appointment, but the doctor couldn't do the appointment because my blood pressure was so high. I explained, "You have no idea who I just talked to!"

As that story demonstrates, I'm still as passionate as ever about hockey. We attend as many games as possible; it's a family thing with us. I'm not a Hockey Mom anymore, though. I've graduated to Hockey Grandma. Yay! With this book, I hope to bring back pleasant memories for all Hockey Moms and perhaps even provide a laugh or two. Enjoy the book!

—Jody M. Anderson,
Hockey Mom

Our Hockey Children

The Shooting Goalie

During a game, a child on the opposing team was skating down to try and score a goal. Our little goalie was too busy to see this guy because he was using his hockey stick as a pretend gun to shoot imaginary ducks!

Yes, the guy scored and won the game for his team.

—Anonymous,
Hockey Mom

Unconditional Love

Child: Mom, would you still love me if I didn't play hockey?

. . . Mom, did you hear me?

Mom: Yes, of course, dear.

Child: You'd still love me?

Mom: No, I meant I heard you.

Child: Well, would you?

Mom: Don't rush me. I'm thinking.

Soccer Mom: When my kids are naughty, I give them a timeout.

Hockey Mom: When my kids are naughty, I put them in the penalty box!

Doctor: Congratulations, it's a girl!

Hockey Mom: Oh, she's so beautiful! She's a blessing. She's a joy. Now put these on her.

Oh, Those Crazy Kids!

Child: Are the lakes frozen yet? Are they?
Are they?

Mom: Sweetie, it's August.

Dad: Son, why do you have black marker
all over your face?

Son: Playoff beard!

Mom: I can't believe you burned down
the garage!

Son: It was an accident,
Mom. I didn't mean to do it.

Mom: I don't care! You're grounded for a
month . . . except to play hockey.

Mom: Yep, now you're a hockey player.

School Days

Suzie: My report today is about Judy Johnson.

Teacher: Suzie, your report is supposed to be about a president.

Suzie: It is. She's president of our Parent Hockey Association.

Teacher: Coach, don't tell me you're already scouting my students. They're only in first grade!

Coach: Well, some of them have potential, but they need to show more focus.

You might be a Hockey Mom if . . . your son always wears a hockey belt, even with a tuxedo.

Mom: You're getting your homework done, right? What are you studying?

Daughter: Um . . . history.

That's Not What Pockets Are For!

Last year, our four-year-old, Tara, started a program that teaches her how to play hockey. I was helping her get ready while my husband, Zac, was loading the dishwasher. As I helped her pull her new pants over her long johns, she realized that the pants had pockets.

She excitedly yelled, "Daddy, now I have a pocket for my lip gloss!"

Zac quickly answered, "No! There's no lip gloss in hockey!"

I guess a girl needs lip gloss, even when she's on the ice.

—Kylah Eckes,
Hockey Mom

Tara: Daddy, now I have a pocket for my lip gloss!

Daddy: No! There's no lip gloss in hockey!

The Hockey Home

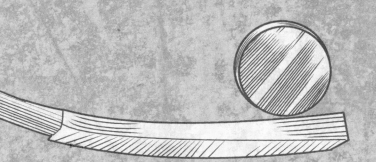

React First, Then Think.

My mom is a full-blooded Yugoslavian, so she's kind of ornery. Most of my memories of her are high-tempered. My mom was one who always reacted and then thought about it afterward. But she was dedicated, committed, giving, and caring. And she always gave you a good meal.

She loved and supported her kids, and she played an important role. She was the head of the household in some ways. Growing up, it was the most important dynamic of the family. She was always there for us. My mom was one of the best—very supportive.

—Mike Peluso,
Hockey Pro
1989–1998

Around the House

Child: Mom, I can't find my skates or my stick!

Mom: Check your bed. Did you sleep with them again?

Mom #1: Hockey sticks are so expensive. I just hate to throw the old ones away.

Mom #2: Well, don't. They have all sorts of uses. You could build a rocking chair with them or use them as pool skimmers. They're great for cleaning out rain gutters. They can be fishing poles, walking sticks, canes . . .

You might be a Hockey Mom if . . . your dust rags are all made from old hockey socks.

Dad: Are you ready to go?

Mom: I don't know. Do you think the earrings are too much?

Dad: Uh, yeah, it's the earrings.

Hockey Kids

Mom #1: Are you going to have more children?

Mom #2: Yes, but we're going to plan it just right. We want our next child to have a good hockey birthday. How about you?

Mom #1: Of course, we want more kids so we can start 'em younger!

Child: Mom, I'm really sorry. I was in the basement, playing around. I hit the puck, and it broke a window.

Mom: Well, did you score?

You might be a Hockey Mom if . . . you've ever said to your child, "No, I don't want to smell your gloves."

Mom: You play hockey?

Boy: Yes, ma'am.

Mom: Keep her out as late as you want.

Acceptable Pet Names

Boards	Bobby
Boxer	Brawler
Breakaway	Checkers
Crease	Dangle
Deke	Easton
Goalie	Goldie
Goon	Gordie
Gretzky	Hat Trick (or Trixie)
Hockey	Icy
Mario	Mullet
Netter	Puck
Skater	Slapshot
Stanley	Winger
Yzerman	Zamboni

You might be a Hockey Mom if . . . you even have to tell your pet to "get out of the way" when there's a hockey game on TV.

What's in the Hockey Bag?

With the kids' school and hockey schedules, life could be a bit crazy as we rushed from one thing to the next.

There was one evening when I received a call from my son Dougie's team manager. He told me that I needed to come to the arena right away. Apparently, when Dougie opened his bag in the locker room, a surprise popped its head out. It was GiGi, our pet ferret!

The team thought it was the best thing to have that cute, furry animal in the locker room. But, unfortunately, GiGi was quite a distraction and needed to go home.

—Joni Zine,
Hockey Mom

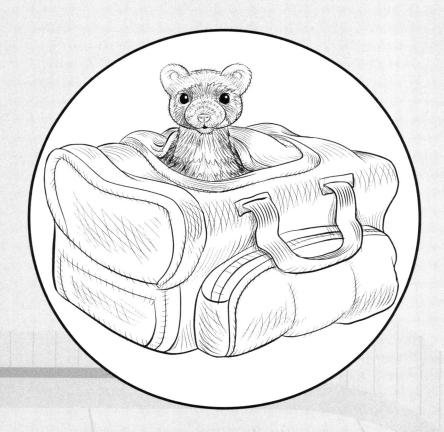

When Dougie opened his bag in the locker
room, a surprise popped its head out.

Family & Friends

Hungry for a Win

The kids were dressed and ready, so on the ice we went. It was game time.

Things were going well, and my shift was over. But for some reason, instead of heading to the bench, I skated over to the glass where my mom was sitting.

I banged on the glass, saying, "Mom, can you get me a hot dog? I'm starving!"

Everyone laughed.

My mother replied, "No! Get back to the bench. You can have one after the game!"

—Alex Reinert,
Hockey Son

Family Antics

Girl: Grandma, I brought my school picture for you.

Grandma: All my friends show me pictures of their granddaughters with pretty dresses and nice makeup. Yours are always hockey pictures.

Girl: Those other girls are sissies, aren't they Grandma?

Mom #1: Are you going to the game this weekend?

Mom #2: I'm not sure. I'll have to see if this is one of the rinks my husband is barred from.

Mom: Are you ready for breakfast, dear?

Dad: It's 4:30 in the morning!

Mom: I'm a Hockey Mom. This is when I always eat.

Social Life

Friend: We should get together some time.
Do you have plans this weekend?

Mom: Practice.

Friend: How about next weekend?

Mom: Practice.

Friend: And the weekend after that?

Mom: Practice . . .

Friend: You're not gonna believe this. I have
two backstage passes to the concert,
and I want you to come with me!

Mom: When's the concert again? I'll need to
check my kids' hockey schedules.

Dad: I know we spend a lot of time with the other parents, but this is ridiculous!

She's No "Hockey Mom"

I grew up in Detroit in the 1940s and '50s. Back in those days, there was no such thing as a Hockey Mom.

My mom wasn't able to be very involved in the sports side of my life. I don't think she saw me play until I was sixteen. But I'll always know that, with my mom's support, I was able to get out and play sports.

—Carl Wetzel,
Hockey Pro
1958–1973

Mom: You can do it! Go! Go! Go!

Stranger: Ma'am, this is a piano recital.

Work & Money

Good Call

I was reffing a game when a team from a big school was beating a much smaller school, 9–1, after two periods. It was a pretty crummy game, actually. Late in the period, the big-school coach asked me if I saw a tripping call.

I said, "What penalty?" I couldn't believe he was worried about a tripping call in a 9–1 game.

He said, "The one down in the corner."

"Was it in front of me or my partner?" I asked.

"In front of your partner," he replied.

I said, "How do you expect me to see that? I'm watching the moms!"

To that, he only answered, "Touche."

—Dave Druk
10-Year District 10
Hockey Official

9 to 5? It's Not a Final Score

Boss: What job are you applying for, Ms. Jones?

Ms. Jones: I'd like to be the president, manager, driver, accountant, fundraiser . . .

Boss: You're a Hockey Mom, aren't you?

Mom: Wow, I had a really busy day at work. I received more than 200 emails!

Dad: How many of them weren't about hockey?

Husband: Why do you always laugh when someone tells you that their kids play soccer?

Cashier: Evenin' ma'am. What'll it be?

Mom: I'll have the usual.

Ah, Technology

Dad: Do you know what time the game starts tonight?

Mom: No, but I can find out. I have the coach on speed dial.

A boss was sitting in his office at work. Every so often, he thought he heard the sound of a hockey goal score. At first, he figured it must be his imagination. But after hearing it for the third time, he stormed out of his office.

"You people should be working, but I can hear someone watching hockey! I want to know who it is," he demanded.

A Hockey Mom in the corner raised her hand. "No one's watching hockey, sir. That's just my cell phone's ring tone."

Mom: Okay, I'll pay for this stuff, but I get half of your first pro contract. Do we have a deal?

The Hockey Psychic

A man at a youth hockey game declared to all the Hockey Moms, "I'm a psychic, and I'll bet any of you a dollar that I can guess your computer password."

Several of the Hockey Moms jumped out of their seats and quickly lined up to take that bet.

The first mom in line waved her dollar bill and said, "Take a guess."

"I'll be happy to," replied the psychic. "But first you must tell me your child's name."

The woman smiled proudly and said, "Tommy Matson."

The man picked up a program and scanned it for a moment. "There he is," said the psychic. "He's number 47, yes?"

The Hockey Mom hesitated, then nodded.

"Your password is hockey47," declared the psychic.

The woman handed him the dollar. Everyone behind her jumped out of line and sat down.

It Costs How Much?

Child: Mom, I need a new hockey stick.

Mom: At those prices, you better have a good reason for needing one.

Child: Mine doesn't have any more goals in it.

Mom: I'll grab my purse.

Banker: Well, ma'am, we can qualify you for a loan of $5,000. Will that be enough?

Mom: No, unfortunately, it won't. I have to pay this year's hockey expenses.

Mom: Get out the checkbook, honey. It's time to pay the big bill again.

Dad: Oh, is the mortgage due?

Mom: No, ice fees.

Mom: And I call this one, "$600 down the drain."

The Dream Home

Jim and Cheri were huge hockey fans. In fact, when they decided to buy a house, they only wanted one that a hockey family had lived in. The realtor took them to view the first house.

Without even going inside, Cheri said, "Nope, not this one."

The realtor brought them to the second house.

Before they entered, Cheri said, "Not this one either."

The realtor was sure they'd love the third house, but without even getting out of her minivan, Cheri said, "No way. A hockey family didn't live here either."

The realtor shrugged. "I don't understand, ma'am. Are you psychic?"

Cheri laughed. "Why on earth would you think that?"

"How else could you know that none of these are hockey homes?"

"Well, did you see the garages?" Cheri answered. "There's not a single puck dent on 'em!"

Mom: How much is the stick you want?

Child: About $180.

Mom: Okay, let's get it.

Child: Should we pick up a birthday card for Dad?

Mom: Are you joking? I'm not spending $5 for that!

Early Bird

My mom is not a morning person, so 6:30 a.m. practices were not her favorite. However, being the best Hockey Mom ever, she always got me there and then took me to Country Kitchen for breakfast prior to school.

Our traditional early-bird breakfast made me late for school, which was a bonus!

I love you, Mom!

—Jeff Nielsen,
Hockey Pro
1994–2001

Girl: A sweatshirt? Thanks, Grandma.

Mom: Unless there's a new hockey team
called the Teddy Bears, we're gonna
have to return that gift.

The Coach
& the Team

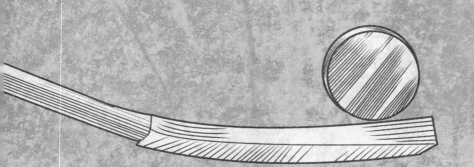

Let's Give Him a Hand

I was watching my son play hockey at the pee-wee level. On his first shift, he was slammed into the corner boards. He finished his shift and went back to the bench, shaking his hand. He took off his glove and sprayed water on his hand. He played the entire game, but every once in a while, he'd shake his hand in pain.

I said to my husband, "Something's wrong with Jeremy's hand."

At the end of the game, he came up the steps, showed me his thumb, and said, "Hey, Mom, I think I broke my thumb."

I took a look, and his thumb was bent the wrong way! I asked him why he didn't tell his coach.

His response was, "If I told him, he wouldn't have let me play."

—Jody M. Anderson,
Hockey Mom

Practice Makes Perfect

Child: Mom, the coach doesn't want you attending practice anymore.

Mom: Why not?

Child: There have been complaints.

Mom: About me? Why?

Child: Because you yell, "Watch this!" to the other parents every time I get the puck.

You might be a Hockey Mom if . . . any time you're away on business, your child must leave a detailed list of instructions for his dad. Otherwise, your husband won't get him to practice on time!

Mom #1: Can . . . you believe . . . it's only . . . 5 a.m.?

Mom #2: There's . . . no place . . . I'd rather . . . be.

Game Time

Mom #1: How come your husband always lets you choose where to sit?

Mom #2: So he can sit on the opposite side of the arena.

Mom #1: What are you doing?

Mom #2: Keeping stats, of course.

Mom #1: But . . . this is practice.

You might be a Hockey Mom if . . . you can name every kid on the ice, but you have no idea who any of your child's classmates are.

Coach: Your kid knows that's just an expression, right?

The Coach's Decisions

Dad: You know he's the coach, right?

Mom: Yes.

Dad: That he's a volunteer?

Mom: Yes.

Dad: That he donates hundreds of hours of his personal time?

Mom: Yes.

Dad: It's still okay to complain about him?

Mom: Yes.

Mom: Coach, I'm calling to complain about my son's ice time last night.

Coach: We only had five kids show up. Your son played the whole game.

Mom: I know, but still . . .

Coach: I hate to tell you this, but the odds of a child making it to the pros are something like one in 100,000.

Mom: Oh, I know. I feel kind of bad for the other 99,999 kids.

Lesson Learned

It was the start of the game, and my son was ready to go. The puck was dropped, and my son and a boy from the other team ran into each other. They both fell, and I laughed.

Then I saw my son get up, and I knew it wasn't going to be good. He was not happy. He swung his stick and hit the kid. Needless to say, he was benched for the remainder of the game.

Afterwards, I walked down to the locker room, and my son was waiting for me. I just looked at him and didn't say a word.

I gave him a hug and told him that I loved him, but the car ride home was a long lesson on what he cannot do in hockey.

—Crystal Ziebarth,
Hockey Mom

Always remember that coaches
have Hockey Moms, too.

On the Road
Again... and Again

Champion!

My son, Derek Plante, was able to experience the ultimate goal of every young hockey player, that of becoming a professional.

In 1999, Derek was traded to Dallas just before the playoffs. They kept winning and pretty soon it was the final round. We drove down to Dallas for the sixth game of the championship series.

The final, winner-take-all game was in Buffalo, which we could not fly to. But we drove up to Des Moines, Iowa, rented a motel room, and watched from there. Dallas won!

The trophy came to our hometown. There was a picture and autograph session at the old high school rink. Then we had a private party for family and friends, and we drank champagne from the cup. I was a very proud mom!

—Anne Gullion,
Hockey Mom

Car Troubles

Mom #1: My husband still drives his car from 1968. It has nearly four hundred thousand miles on it!

Mom #2: That's nothin'. I have an '04 SUV . . . and I'm a Hockey Mom!

Mom #1: How old are your children?

Mom #2: I have a '90 and a '93. And you?

Mom #1: A '95 and a '97.

You might be a Hockey Mom if . . . your children think locker rooms smell like your car.

Mom: I don't know, dear. Do you think we'll ever find the right vehicle?

Dad: What's wrong with this one?

Mom: It's not big enough!

Family Vacation

Dad: There's a hockey tournament in Wisconsin Dells. You know what that means, right?

Mom: Family vacation!

Dad: You know, you're not very good at giving people directions.

Mom: Why? Because I'm a woman?

Mom: No, because your directions are always based on the closest hockey arena.

You might be a Hockey Mom if . . . there's a hockey arena in the background of all your family pictures.

It must be hockey season.

Free Time

Mom: I feel totally lost. I don't know what to do. Life seems to have no meaning anymore!

Dad: It sounds like you're having a mid-life crisis.

Mom: No, I just have a free weekend.

Mom: I always wanted to garden.

Dad: Then why don't you?

Mom: The kids aren't gonna drive themselves to those hockey camps!

You might be a Hockey Mom if . . . you've had to deal with three children, three tournaments, three different towns—all on the same day.

Stranger #1: Are those people crazy? It's freezing out here.

Stranger #2: They must be in town for the big hockey tournament.

The Broken Nose

I'll never forget the time I broke my nose at Madison Square Garden in New York. My trainer had to put two of the long, skinny, white tubes up my nostrils in order to stop the bleeding. Later, they put me up on the jumbo video board with those two cotton things hanging out of my nose.

Apparently they put me on TV too because my mom called me right after the game to make sure I was alright. I was getting asked for a week after if I was okay, so my mom wasn't the only one who saw me on TV looking all beat up!

My mom was always willing to drop everything and drive anywhere at a moment's notice. She was—and still is—awesome!

—Derek Plante,
Hockey Pro
1993–2008

Doctor: Ma'am, I'm sorry to inform you that your son's leg is broken.

Mom: Well, can he skate on it?

Holidays & Special Events

Whoops! That's Not My Kid.

I can picture my father yelling over the front seat of the car, but my mom was a calming influence. She'd say things like, "You weren't bad. Everything was good." She evened out my dad.

I also remember Parents' Night in Duluth, Minnesota. My mom got out of sequence, and she started walking out in front of the crowd with the wrong player. That was embarrassing for her, and she had to hurry back and find me!

I thank my mom for raising me with the morals and values that she instilled in me, which shaped me as a hockey player. If I was afraid to tell my mom about it, I knew I shouldn't be doing it. It helped me to make good decisions and to be a leader on the team for the guys.

—Sean Toomey,
Hockey Pro
1986–1989

Holidays

Mom: I learned the strangest thing today.

Dad: Oh, really? What's that?

Mom: Thanksgiving is actually a holiday. It's not just a tournament.

Mom: Are you excited for Christmas?

Child: I think so. Is Christmas home or away this year?

Mom: I hate sending Christmas cards.

Dad: Why? Because we never have a good family picture?

Mom: No, because the stats only show half the season!

Stocking stuffers.

Special Events

Guest: Where's your son? I wanted to congratulate him on his first communion.

Mom: Sorry, he couldn't be here today.

Guest: But this is his big day! Where else could he be?

Mom: There's a hockey game.

Principal: Mrs. Smith, what can I do for you?

Mom: I'm wondering if we can reschedule graduation this year.

Principal: What on earth for?

Mom: Hockey tryouts. My child got a second call back.

Mom: What are you supposed to be?

Child: A hockey ref.

Mom: Wow, that is scary.

Mom's Permission

Dear Mr. Rudy,

Please excuse Jeremy's absence from school yesterday. That new hockey movie was released in theaters, and he couldn't wait to see it.

Sincerely,

Jeremy's Mom

Dad: I don't understand. Why do you get so lonely during the off-season?

Mom: I miss the other parents!

You might be a Hockey Mom if . . . you can identify your children's Christmas gifts by shape.

Mom: Honey, I didn't think your tux was right for prom. I got you this one instead.

Early Mornings

When I think of my mom as a Hockey Mom, I think of her waking me up on those freezing cold, early Saturday mornings to take me to my 7 a.m. game. She'd make my breakfast and try as hard as she could to tie my skates as tight as my dad could. When we had a weekend tournament, she knew that we needed to eat right, so she'd spend all day making meals for me and my brother.

My mom always taught me to show respect for others—especially adults. That translated into me having a good respect for the other players on the ice. My mom is a great woman. She was always there when I needed her. She was and still is someone I can talk to about anything. I love her so much, my mom, Karen Fata!

—Rico Fata,
Hockey Pro
1998–Present

Mom: Say, "Hockey." You can do it. Yes, you can. "Hockey."

Busy Chatting

Although my mom loved to watch me play, she never did much watching during the games. She loves to interact and be social. Oftentimes, I'd be talking about a game with my dad, and my mom would mention, "I missed that goal." That's because she was busy chatting away with another mom—or whoever was sitting next to her!

I would not have been successful in hockey without my mom's support and guidance. She played a supportive and emotional role, always making sure that hockey was fun for me and that I enjoyed it. There was no better feeling than to know that my mom was there to guide me, on and off the ice. I'm grateful for all the time, energy, and money that she put in so that I could play hockey.

—Natalie Darwitz,
Women's Hockey Olympian
2002, 2006, 2010

Appreciate Your Opportunities

My mom, Marlene Brodt, taught me how to skate when I was 18 months old. She spent hours at open skating, holding me up on my skates. When I started playing hockey with the boys (there was no girls' hockey then), she spent much of her time driving me and my siblings to practices and to games.

Although my mom is very athletic, there were limited opportunities for women in sports for most of her youth. She began playing recreational hockey when she was in her twenties and still plays today in her sixties. She taught me to never take my opportunities for granted, and I hope that I'm able to continue playing and enjoying the game for years to come. She is the definition of a dedicated Hockey Mom.

—Winny Brodt Brown,
Women's Hockey Pro
2004–Present

An Interview with Mike Eruzione

When you think of your mom as a Hockey Mom, what comes to mind?

She's somebody who didn't really get involved.

Oh, not like some of the Hockey Moms today?

Very, very opposite of the Hockey Moms today. My mother would take me to practice, drop me off, go home, and come back and get me. I remember one tournament during my Boston University days. We were playing in the Final Four—now called the Frozen Four—against St. Louis. My mother flew out, but she never watched the game. She sat in the bathroom, she was so nervous! In between periods, she would go out and see how we were doing.

And making sure you weren't hurt?

You know, it's funny, one time in prep school I got hit in the face with a stick. It came up and cut me in my forehead, and my mother was right at the end of the rink. I was bleeding and blood was coming down my face. So I skated to the bench and started to wipe the blood off. My mother came out of the stands and behind the bench to see if I was okay. I looked at her and said, "Don't ever do that." She looked at me and then went up in the stands. After the game, my father said, "If I ever hear you talk to your mother like that during a game, you'll be in big trouble." And I ended up getting 10 stitches in my forehead.

Were there any traditions before a game? Like, was your family into the pastas and all of that kind of stuff?

When I was real young, my mother used to give me oranges. She was kind of the "Orange Lady" for the team. She had this little bucket, and she used to cut me oranges. I would take them in the car, and in between periods or after the game, we would have oranges to eat.

How did your mom help to shape you as a hockey player?

There was a ton of support. I played hockey, football, and baseball. My mom was always there for me and supported me. She was always at my games, and she was like that with my brothers, although my sisters weren't into sports. But you know, if I needed something, she seemed to find a way to get it.

We didn't grow up with a lot of money, so it was always hard for me. I remember we would have to pay 50 cents to skate at the practice in the morning. Sometimes I didn't have the 50 cents, so I would owe the 50 cents. But the next week, my mom would always find a way to get me a dollar, so I could pay last week and the next week.

I remember after the Olympics, a reporter was at my house doing a story on me. The guy looked at

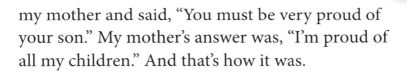

my mother and said, "You must be very proud of your son." My mother's answer was, "I'm proud of all my children." And that's how it was.

When I was at Boston University, we had a lot of Canadians on the team and very few Americans. I would have the team come over for dinner. We would take my mother's bed apart and move chairs and tables in there, and my mother would make dinner for the whole team.

When I was playing once in Toledo, Ohio, my mother made dinner in Boston for eight of us, froze it, put it on the plane, brought it to Toledo, and served dinner for the team.

Then in Lake Placid, the parents all stayed in a house. (We called it the hostage house.) My mom made dinner for all the parents. Mr. Christian drove all over Lake Placid to find cheese so my mother could make lasagna. She was very involved with all the parents.

Since your mother couldn't watch your college tournaments, was she there watching the Olympic games?

She went to one game. She flew up, and all night long she got caught in a snowstorm in Washington, DC. It was a nightmare for her, but she got into Lake Placid. She watched the Russian game and then flew out the next day.

Did you even get to see her?

Yes, I did get to see her because after we beat the Russians, they interviewed me in the street. My mother was standing next to me, and my father was standing next to me. It was me, my mom and dad, Jim Craig, and Jim Craig's father. They interviewed us, and it was kind of comical because my mother just stood there and didn't say a word.

Did she think you could win? Was she pretty confident in the team?

We never talked about it. It was always just, "Congratulations," you know, "Good luck," and that was about it.

Thank you. I appreciate you giving me some of your time for this interview.

Okay, excellent, thank you very much.

Mike Eruzione was the captain of the 1980 Winter Olympics United States national hockey team. He and his team famously defeated the Soviet Union in the "Miracle on Ice" game, on their way to a gold medal.

About the Author

Jody M. Anderson grew up on a 100-acre Quarter Horse farm, where she boarded, trained, showed and bred horses. Expensive, time-consuming and with lots of driving, she now knows that this prepared her for life as a Hockey Mom!

Jody has four children, five grandchildren and one husband. They are the loves of her life. One child played lacrosse in college, another was a diver in college, one played hockey at JR level and one at HS level.

Jody's family still enjoys going to professional hockey games and cheering on the local team. Best of all, Jody now has the privilege of watching her grandchildren play hockey. Life is fabulous!

Follow Jody @Minnesota_Wild on Twitter. Read her blog at HockeyMomsArentCrazy.com.